SKATEBOARDING
TIPS AND TRICKS™

RIDING STREET
COURSES

**PETER MICHALSKI
AND JUSTIN HOCKING**

rosen publishing's
rosen
central®

Published in 2017 by The Rosen Publishing Group, Inc.
29 East 21st Street, New York, NY 10010

Library of Congress Cataloging-in-Publication Data

Names: Michalski, Pete. | Hocking, Justin.
Title: Riding street courses / Peter Michalski and Justin Hocking.
Description: First Edition. | New York : Rosen Central, 2017. | Series:
  (Skateboarding Tips and Tricks) | Includes bibliographical references and
  index. | Audience: Grades: 7-12.
Identifiers: LCCN 2016008905| ISBN 9781477788769 (Library Bound) | ISBN
  9781477788745 (Paperback) | ISBN 9781477788752 (6-pack)
Subjects: LCSH: Skateboarding--Juvenile literature.
Classification: LCC GV859.8 .M544 2017 | DDC 796.22--dc23
LC record available at http://lccn.loc.gov/2016008905

Manufactured in China

CONTENTS

INTRODUCTION   4

CHAPTER ONE
STREET COURSES   6

CHAPTER TWO
STARTING OUT: BASIC TRICKS   14

CHAPTER THREE
THE NEXT LEVEL: INTERMEDIATE
        TRICKS   24

CHAPTER FOUR
ADVANCED STREET TRICKS   32

GLOSSARY   40
FOR MORE INFORMATION   42
FOR FURTHER READING   44
BIBLIOGRAPHY   45
INDEX   46

INTRODUCTION

If you love to skateboard, you are not alone. Millions of your fellow skaters are out there, all around the world, taking it to the streets and the skateparks. Skating has never been more popular.

Nor has it ever been so easy to get out there and do it. Plenty of skaters use the already existing built environment to their advantage. Even better, growing public support has helped many communities everywhere build new skateparks. Chances are that your local skatepark probably has some kind of street course in it, or at least a few common street-style obstacles. These are the parts of a skatepark that imitate the obstacles skaters encounter on regular streets and sidewalks, like ledges, curbs, and handrails.

One major benefit of street courses versus skating on public streets is the ability to focus and not have to worry about traffic, pedestrians, or the occasional angry business and property owners. You may already have noticed many such people who may not be open to having their private property (or even the public space near them) used by skaters. Nationwide, police also seem to have mixed responses to skating.

Perhaps you have developed some skating skills already and have even taken a shot at riding

A skater slides her board along the top of a rail, one of the typical structures found in skatepark street courses. Riding street courses is one of the most popular genres of skateboarding.

around a street course near you. However well you skate already, this book will provide a refresher for already seasoned skaters and plenty of tips and useful information for newbies. From basic through medium and intermediate tricks, to more advanced and technical ones, this book will help you take your street skating skills to another level. Regardless of whether you progress quickly or take your time, remember to, above all, have fun.

CHAPTER ONE

STREET COURSES

There is nothing quite like skating on the street. There is something free and spontaneous about it, tackling new obstacles as you go and finding previously undiscovered skate spots.

Things not originally designed for skating, like stairs, handrails, ledges, the curb, and the street itself, become prime territory for challenging yourself and trying out new tricks. It lets you be creative and envision your environment in a way that non-skaters usually don't. Street skating can be thought of as creating a new and personalized skatepark wherever you go.

But there are lots of risks involved, too. You might get hassled by people who don't want you skating on their property. And if you get hurt, there might not be anyone around to take care of you. For lots of people, these risks only add to the thrill of street skating. For many riders of earlier eras, one of the lures was the rebellion and indepedence of skating. Nowdays, skating is more a mainstream sport and pastime, and less so the rebellious activity of the late 20th century.

DISCOVERING STREET COURSES

With all the positive aspects of street skating, you might wonder why you should bother with street courses in a skatepark at all. They're designed to resemble actual "street spots" like stairs, ledges, and handrails, but they're not the real thing. And you sometimes have to wait in line and pay a fee to skate. Street courses sometimes get really crowded, too, so you'll have to wait your turn and watch out for other skaters, which can get frustrating.

But skating in street courses has a lot of benefits, too. As skatepark construction technology improves, some truly

Before street courses—and skateparks in general—were widely built and became popular, the most common venues most skaters took advantage of were their local sidewalks and streets.

incredible and spacious street courses are being built in places like Chandler, Arizona, and Louisville, Kentucky. Packed with perfectly shaped quarter-pipes (ramps that are half of a half-pipe); long, smooth ledges; and uniquely shaped rails, you won't find these kinds of extraordinary concrete wonderlands on any random street. This new generation of street course allows skaters to hit a number of different obstacles in one run, linking trick after trick after trick.

Also, if you're interested in skateboarding competitively, most street contests actually take place in skatepark street courses. One of the biggest and most famous street contests takes place at the Skate Park of Tampa (S.P.O.T.). Every year S.P.O.T. organizes an amateur contest, and thousands of "young guns" from all over the country come just to enter. This is a proving ground for younger skaters seeking sponsorship by a company and hoping to move up in the ranks of the skate world.

Most skaters, though, don't take contests too seriously. No one really wants to "beat" another skater like players would in a basketball or football game. Most people enter just to do their best and to get a chance to hang out with other skaters. That's the other reason skateparks are great—they're a centralized meeting place where you can join up with your friends or meet new people. Finally, street courses are generally safer than street skating. There's usually someone around to help you if you get hurt. And while you have to deal with lots of other skaters, you won't have to worry about getting hassled by police or property owners.

The truth is, skating in the actual streets and skating in street courses are both a lot of fun. Just because you do one doesn't mean you can't do the other. In fact, doing both will help you become a more well-rounded skateboarder.

Here is a typical street course in a skatepark. Note how many of its elements—including the rails, quarter-pipe, stairs, and other structures—imitate the built landscape of the streets and parks that street skaters encounter.

THE STREET COURSE ENVIRONMENT

Street courses come in all sizes and shapes, and no two are exactly alike. Some are indoors; some are outdoors. Some are made of wood, and others are made entirely of cement. Some have lots of quarter-pipes and "transitions" (another word for the curving part of a ramp), while others have mostly ledges and other "flat" obstacles. But there are a few elements that you will find in just about every street course:

- Pyramids: Pyramids are made up of several banks connected together to form the shape of an actual pyramid (except most skatepark pyramids have a flat top instead of the pointy tip you see in Egyptian pyramids).
- Banks: Banks are flat, slanted obstacles, like ramps without the curve. Banks help you maintain speed in a street course by going down them. They are a good place to try some more technical tricks.
- Ledges: Ledges are square, boxlike obstacles that are good for grinds and slides. Most ledges are made out of concrete, but some are a combination of wood and metal. They're generally between half a foot and three feet (fifteen centimeters and one meter tall).
- Manual Pads: Sometimes known as a "wheelie," a manual is a trick where you ride balancing only on your back wheels (unless you're doing a "nose manual," where you balance only on your front wheels). Manual pads are small, flat boxes that you ollie onto and then manual across.
- Rails: Rails are similar to ledges, but they're made out of metal. A "flat bar" is a type of small, flat rail, while a handrail is a bigger type of rail that usually descends down a set of stairs.
- Quarter-Pipes: A quarter-pipe is a type of ramp with a transition. Like banks, quarter-pipes also help you maintain your speed. They're also good for all sorts of tricks such as grinds, stalls, and airs.

A skater grinds down a ledge in a skatepark. Many elements of skatepark street courses replicate elements found in other public places, such as parks, office parks, and the street itself.

SOME OF AMERICA'S BEST STREET COURSES

- **Louisville Extreme Park (Louisville, Kentucky):** One of the largest outdoor public skateparks in the world, the Louisville park features a gigantic concrete street course area, with a large variety of banks, ledges, manual pads, etc. Stadium-style lighting allows this unique park to remain open twenty-four hours a day.
- **Rye Airfield (Rye, New Hampshire):** This enormous indoor skatepark boasts over 50,000 square feet (4,645 square meters) of skateable terrain. By offering three separate street courses—for beginner, intermediate, and advanced skaters—this park has something for skaters of all abilities. The advanced street course area also features a unique rainbow-shaped ledge.
- **Skate Park of Tampa (Tampa, Florida):** Though the street course in the Tampa park is relatively small, it's filled with modern, skater-built pyramids, ledges, quarter-pipes, etc. This makes it the perfect spot for the famous annual Skate Park of Tampa amateur and pro contests.
- **Fossil Creek Skate Park (Fort Collins, Colorado):** Unlike many street courses that feature quarter-pipes and other curved surfaces that you rarely find at an actual street spot, the Fossil Creek Skate Park was designed to look like an actual urban plaza, with staircases and ledges of varying sizes. The park also features a very unique "gap" where advanced skaters can jump over a small reservoir that's actually filled with water!

WATCHING AND LEARNING—SAFELY

If you read this book carefully and put in some major practice time, you'll pick up most of the tricks we cover. Unfortunately, we can only cover a handful of tricks, even though there are hundreds more to try and many different ways of doing each individual trick, depending on the type of obstacle you hit. So an equally important way to learn about skateboarding is to actually watch other people in action.

If you are new to skating street courses, when you show up at one, it's best to try to ease in rather than drop in right away. It might be best to sit back and just check things out for awhile. You can learn much simply by watching the better and advanced skaters. Notice how they use the obstacles on the street course, what kind of lines they take, and how they start and end tricks. Even watching how they recover from tricks they don't land can be educational. It can also help you prevent injuries, which are most common for beginners.

Going in smart will do a whole lot more for your skating development than having a collision with someone else the first time in—an event that will likely not make you an army of friends at the skatepark, either.

The other main precaution to take is to always gear up: wear a helmet and pads. Not all skateparks require them. Some do, but do not feel embarrassed or ashamed to sport them even if they are not required. It's just smart skating.

CHAPTER TWO

STARTING OUT: BASIC TRICKS

Before embarking on some serious street course skating, it is a good idea to have some fundamentals down. Knowing how to ollie, do a manual, and maybe even kickflips and some other simple tricks will help you build a street course repertoire quicker. With these basics learned, you will be better prepared to start perfecting these tricks on street course obstacles. This will lead, down the line, to more advanced tricks.

The tricks in this book are divided into three categories: basic, intermediate, and advanced. It's important to start out with the basics, like learning to ollie on a pyramid, because you'll need to have that down before you try harder moves like a frontside 360 ollie, which is a more difficult form of the basic ollie. That's how skateboarding works—it's a constant progression where learning one trick gives you the foundation for learning something else. But don't worry about getting the hardest tricks down. Skateboarding is really just about having fun and moving at your own pace.

DOING AN OLLIE ON A PYRAMID

Most street courses have some sort of pyramid, and they're often the centerpiece of the course. Pyramids are a popular place for more technical flip tricks (we'll cover these later in the book), which require you to know how to ollie, so it's good to learn a basic ollie first.

1. Head toward the pyramid at a slight angle with a moderate amount of speed.

A skater is caught in this mid-air photograph while executing a kickflip over a graffiti-covered pyramid in a skatepark.

2. As you ride up the side of the pyramid, bend your knees deeply and stay low. To do the best ollie, move your front foot back behind your front truck bolts and stay on the balls of your feet and toes.
3. As you reach the pyramid's peak, jump up and snap the tail of your skateboard on the ground as you would for a regular ollie in the street.
4. When you reach your maximum height in the air above the pyramid, tuck your knees up toward your body and use your feet to lift the board up as high as you can.
5. Spot your landing, straighten your legs out, and set the board back down. Bend your knees as you land to absorb the shock.

OLLIE TO FAKIE ON A BANK

Doing a trick to "fakie" means you ride away backward. Flat banks are a good place to do more technical tricks, so it's good to learn some bank basics first like ollie to fakie. Try these on a small, shallow bank first, and then work it up to steeper, taller banks.

1. Ride up the bank with your knees bent.
2. Just before you reach the top, ollie up above, or higher than, the top of the bank.
3. As you begin to land, try to set your front and back wheels down at the same time. Put a little extra weight on your front foot as you land. Keep your shoulders straight, and as you start to roll backward down the bank, simply turn your neck and head ninety degrees, so you can see where you're going.

A skater ollies big over a tall bank.

4. Bend your knees and stay low as you roll down and back onto the flat surface.

50-50 GRIND ON A LEDGE

This is the first trick that most people learn on a ledge. You can try it on a small curb first, and then work your way up to higher ledges. When you're first getting the hang of the 50-50, you don't need much speed. But once you get comfortable, rolling up to the ledge with more speed will help you grind faster and farther.

1. Approach the ledge with moderate speed and at a slight angle. You should be on the balls of your feet and your toes, and your front foot should be back behind your truck bolts for maximum snap in your ollie.
2. Get really low and then ollie up to the ledge. Guide your board into place, so that you set both trucks down on the edge of the ledge.
3. Bend your knees slightly, and keep your hips and shoulders parallel to the ledge as you grind.
4. As you reach the end of the ledge, put a little extra weight on your heels, press down slightly on your tail, and lift your front trucks off. Set the board down smoothly on the ground, and bend your knees to absorb the shock.

OLLIE TO MANUAL ON A MANUAL PAD

As we mentioned before, a manual in the street is like a "wheelie," where you roll while balancing on your back wheels only, with your front wheels up in the air. They're easy on the flat ground, but it takes more skill to ollie into a manual on a street obstacle.

Try this trick on smaller manual pads first, and then work your way up to higher ones.

1. Roll toward the manual pad with your knees bent. You can gauge how much speed you need depending on how long the manual pad is.
2. Ollie up onto the manual pad.
3. As you land on the top, put extra weight on your back foot. Your back knee should be slightly bent as you press down on the tail to keep your front trucks up in the "manual" position. Use your front foot to balance and hold the position, and try not to drag your tail on the manual pad.
4. As you roll off the end of the manual pad, press down slightly on your tail, but don't snap your tail on the ground like you would for an ollie. Once you land back on the ground, set

This skater is executing a manual on a manual pad.

your front wheels down and bend your knees a little as you ride away.

FRONTSIDE BOARDSLIDE ON A FLAT BAR

The frontside boardslide is one of the more difficult beginner tricks. It's a classic trick that looks stylish when done right. When you're first learning, try sliding just the last foot (thirty cm) or so of a short flat bar. Once you get more confident with this trick, approach the bar with more speed to slide the entire length of the bar.

1. As you roll up toward the flat bar with medium speed, your chest and body should be directly facing the obstacle, with your shoulders parallel to it.
2. As you reach the middle of the bar, snap an ollie, turning the board ninety degrees in the direction toward your toes. Make sure you ollie high enough to get your front trucks and wheels over the bar.
3. Land with your board balanced on the bar. If you have enough speed, your board will slide on the bar. Keep your shoulders perpendicular to the rail and rotate your head and neck so you can look over your lead shoulder. Looking over your shoulder helps keep your weight forward (and to avoid the temptation to lean backward), which makes it easier to come off.
4. As you reach the end of the flat bar, put some weight on your tail and use your front foot and your body to turn the board ninety degrees toward your heels. Try to set your front and back wheels down at the same time and ride away smoothly.

DROPPING IN ON A QUARTER-PIPE

Start out on a smaller quarter-pipe, one that's about four or five feet (1.2 or 1.5 m) high. Make sure no one's in the way when you first drop in. This is a good one to learn before you move on, because dropping in on a ramp helps you get the speed you'll need for some of the more advanced tricks.

PLAYING S.K.A.T.E.

So now you have a few tricks down in the street course, right? If so, you're ready to play a few rounds of S.K.A.T.E. To play, you need at least two other friends who are at about the same skating skill level as yourself. It's also a good idea to play S.K.A.T.E. when the skatepark isn't too crowded, or you might end up getting in people's way.

You play S.K.A.T.E. pretty much the same way you play H.O.R.S.E. with a basketball. First, you have to establish an order, so that the same person always goes first, second, third, etc. Once you're ready to go, the first skater rides into the street course and does the trick of his/her choice. If the first skater makes the trick, then the second skater has to do the exact same trick. If the second skater makes it, the third skater has to do it, too. It goes on like this until someone misses the trick, which gives him a her an "S." Then it starts all over, and the next skater gets to set a trick.

As soon as anyone gets all five of the letters—S.K.A.T.E.—he's out. The winner of the game is the last person left.

A skater drops in on a quarterpipe that has been temporarily constructed as part of a skate competition in a downtown area.

1. Set your tail down on the coping of the ramp with the trucks and wheels hanging over the edge. Place your back foot on the tail to keep the board in place. Keep your knees bent slightly.
2. Slowly move your front foot forward, keeping most of your weight on your back foot. Rest your front foot at a slight forward angle over your front bolts, and keep your knees bent.
3. Now begin to lean forward, getting your hips out over the board and shifting much of your weight from your back foot to your front foot. Keep your shoulder tucked a little bit as you lean forward, and avoid the urge to lean backward. As your hips begin to move forward, straighten your front leg out some and press down firmly with your front foot, pushing the nose of your board down into the ramp so that your front wheels make solid contact with the transition.
4. Keep your knees bent slightly as you ride down the quarter-pipe and into the street course. Make sure to look out for other skaters. Congratulations on your first drop in!

CHAPTER THREE

THE NEXT LEVEL: INTERMEDIATE TRICKS

From nailing and landing basic tricks, there's nowhere to go but up. You are now ready for some more difficult tricks to perform on a street course. Most of these build directly on the skills explored before. Getting these down will get you even closer to more impressive—and more importantly, even more fun—advanced street course maneuvers.

FRONTSIDE 180 OLLIE ON A PYRAMID

To do this trick, you should be comfortable doing 180 ollies on the flat ground. This is a fun trick, and it's a good one to learn before you try the more advanced frontside 360 ollie.

1. Approach the pyramid the same way you would for a normal ollie. For this trick, it sometimes helps to hang your front toe off the edge of the board just slightly.
2. Snap your tail to ollie just as you reach the pyramid's peak. As you rise in the air, begin to shift your hips and

shoulder around 180 degrees, or half a circle, and use your front foot to guide the board round. At the same time, tuck your knees up toward your body like you would for a normal ollie.

3. As you begin to land, your hips and shoulders should be turned all the way around, so that your back shoulder faces forward. Make sure to get your head around, so that you're looking over your back shoulder as you land.

4. Try to set your front and back wheels down at the same time when you land. Upon landing, place a little more weight on your front foot (which is now your back foot, since you're rolling backward). Roll down the pyramid and get ready for the next trick.

KICKFLIP TO FAKIE ON A FLAT BANK

To do this trick, you need to have know-how to do kickflips. Also, make sure to warm up with a few simple ollie to fakies on the bank.

1. Roll up the bank with your knees bent slightly. Stay on the balls of your feet and your toes.

2. The secret to this trick is to make the board kick-flip while you're on your way up the bank, rather than waiting until your momentum is coming back down. So just before you reach the top of the bank, pop your tail as you would in a normal ollie and flick the edge of the board with the side of your foot, just like for a kickflip in the street.

3. Tuck your knees up a bit as the board flips—this makes it easier to catch the board with your feet.

4. After you catch the board, set it back down with a little extra weight on your front foot. Look over your back shoulder and stay low as you roll down.

TAILSLIDE ON A LEDGE

You should have 50-50s down before you try tailslides. This is another good trick to learn on a curb first.

1. Roll up to the ledge the same way you would for a 50-50. You'll have to ollie even higher than you would for a 50-50, though, so stay on the balls of your feet and your toes, and get low before you pop your tail.

A boarder executes a tailslide on a ledge in a skatepark's street course.

2. As you snap your ollie, quickly turn your hips and shoulders ninety degrees away from the ledge. Lift your back leg up high to get the tail above the ledge.
3. Lock your tail on the top of the ledge. To make the board slide, lean forward and push the tail along with your back foot.
4. As you begin to slow down or reach the end of the ledge, turn your board off with your front foot and by rotating your hips and shoulders ninety degrees back toward the ledge. Set the board back down and ride away.

NOSE MANUAL ON A MANUAL PAD

Make sure you're comfortable with nose manuals in the street before trying it on a manual pad. This one takes a lot of balance and finesse, so don't get frustrated if it takes a while to learn.

1. Approach the manual pad at fairly low speed.
2. Snap your ollie, and as you drift up onto the manual pad, move your front foot forward so that it rests just in front of your truck bolts and in the "pocket" where the nose of your board begins to curve upward.
3. Keep your weight forward as you land on your front wheels only. Use the ball of your foot and toes to maintain your balance on the front wheels as you manual across the manual pad. Your back leg should be bent.
4. As you reach the end of the manual pad, press down on the nose and lift your tail to avoid dragging your back trucks as you pop off.

A skater does a nose manual in the skatepark that lies underneath Queen Elizabeth Hall in London, England.

HALF-CAB BOARDSLIDE ON A FLAT BAR

You should already be comfortable with backside boardslides before you try this trick. And you should be able to do a half-cab ollie on the street. You should also be comfortable riding in the fakie position when you try this one.

1. Push up to the flat bar with your board and body facing backward. As you ride up, your shoulders should be roughly parallel to the bar, and your head and neck should be turned so you can look over your back shoulder.
2. Pop your ollie and begin to turn your hips and shoulders ninety degrees. Guide the board around with your front foot and set it down on the bar.
3. Stay forward as your board slides on the bar.
4. As you reach the end, continue to rotate your shoulders and hips around, and use your feet to turn off the bar. You should come all the way around and ride off going forward again.

A QUIZ ON SKATEBOARD TRIVIA

Skateboarding has a long and interesting history. Try to guess some of the following trivia questions. Once you learn the answers, impress your friends with your new skate knowledge.

1. **Which pro skater invented the ollie?**
2. **Which pro skater was the first to do an ollie down the twenty-foot- (six-meter-) high "leap of faith"?**

(continued on the next page)

(continued from the previous page)

3. One of the most famous street spots ever was called Love Park. In which East Coast city was Love Park located?
4. Who invented the kickflip?
5. Who holds the world record for highest air on a ramp (18 feet, or 5.5 m)?
6. Who is the only pro skater to land a 900-degree spin on a vert ramp?
7. Who was the first professional female street skater?
8. Who invented "The McTwist"?
9. What professional skater is nicknamed "TNT"?
10. What do you call the trick where the grip-tape side of your board slides on the ledge, while you stand on the bottom of the board?

ANSWERS:

1. Alan Gelfand
2. Jamie Thomas
3. Philadelphia
4. Rodney Mullen
5. Danny Way
6. Tony Hawk
7. Elissa Steamer
8. Mike McGill
9. Tony Trujillo
10. The dark slide

AXLE STALL ON A QUARTER-PIPE

"Axle" is another name for your truck, so when you do an axle stall, you rest, or stall, your trucks on the top of the coping, rather than grinding. Axle stalls are a good "set-up" trick—they give you a chance to rest for just a moment, and then get plenty of speed as you drop back into the quarter-pipe.

1. Ride straight up the quarter-pipe. You need some extra speed to get all the way on top of the deck.
2. As you reach the top of the ramp, press down on your tail and lift up your front trucks so that they avoid hitting the coping.
3. Set your back truck on the coping first, putting some extra weight on your back heel so you can get your board and body all the way up on the deck.

A skater does a boardslide, a maneuver that can be executed on nearly any structure in a skatepark street course, including quarter-pipes.

4. Once your back truck is resting on the coping, use it as your pivot point, bringing your shoulders and hips around so they're parallel with the coping below you. Set your front trucks down, keeping the weight on your heels and your body leaning in toward the ramp.
5. After you stall for a second, press down on your tail with the toes of your back foot, lean forward, turn off the coping, and ride back into the ramp.

CHAPTER FOUR

ADVANCED STREET TRICKS

etting some beginner and intermediate tricks under your belt—some slides, grinds, and flips—maybe took a little effort, but it was well worth it. That will seem like the easy part when you undertake your next mission: advanced tricks on the street course. You may have gotten some of your earlier tricks down in a few days or so. But the higher-level, technical ones take longer, some of them weeks or even months to get the hang of, much less perfect them. Skateboarding is not always easy, but you will find it more than worthwhile, once you have gotten the hang of things.

FRONTSIDE 360 OLLIE ON A PYRAMID

To do this trick, you should definitely be comfortable with frontside 180 ollies on a pyramid. The secret to this difficult trick is to "wind up", or prepare to turn your body one full circle, before you start your spin.

1. As you approach the pyramid, bend your knees and "wind up" your body by turning your shoulders and

torso just slightly in the opposite direction of your spin. This "counter-rotation" will give you the momentum to complete the 360-degree turn. Also, your front foot should be pretty far back from the nose, with your front toe hanging slightly off the board.

2. Ride up the pyramid, almost parallel with the pyramid's "ridge." Pop your tail and spring up in the air while whipping your shoulders and hips around.

3. Use the side of your front foot to guide the board around 360 degrees. Make sure to get your head and shoulders all the way around, so that you're looking straight ahead as you land.

4. Complete your spin, set the board back down, and bend your knees slightly as you roll away.

BLUNTSLIDE ON A LEDGE

Bluntslides are the most difficult of all the ledge tricks. Try these on a regular curb before you attempt it on a ledge.

1. Ride up the ledge at a slight angle, the same way you

It is better to try bluntslides on lower structures when you are first learning.

would for a backside 50-50. You need a lot of speed for this one.

2. Snap a big ollie, high enough to get your back wheels all the way up on top of the ledge.

3. As you land on the ledge, shift all your weight to your back foot, and push your tail against the edge of the ledge. Keep your front wheels and nose up in the air. If you have enough speed, you'll slide on your tail with your back wheels on top of the ledge.

4. One of the hardest things about the bluntslide is landing. As you reach the end of the ledge, you actually have to do a slight ollie out of the bluntslide position. Put a little extra pressure on your tail, and press down on the front of the board slightly. Then use your back foot to pop the board off the ledge and level it out, while turning your shoulders and hips to face forward.

KICKFLIP TO MANUAL ON A MANUAL PAD

This is a good one to try once you have kickflips and manuals wired. And you can try adding variations as you roll off the manual pad, like a 180 ollie, a pop shove-it, or even another kickflip. Keep in mind that these kinds of technical manual tricks are really difficult and may take you countless tries to learn.

1. Roll up to the manual pad the same way you would for a regular manual.

2. Just like with a normal kickflip, you have to slide your foot up the front of the board as you ollie, and "flick" the edge

A skater is shown in midair doing a kickflip. The position of the board will right itself due to its momentum.

of the board to make it flip. You'll have to ollie a little higher than usual to get up on the manual pad.

3. Try to catch the board with your back foot first. This makes it easier to put a little extra weight on your tail, which will put you in the manual position as you land on the manual pad.
4. Manual across the manual pad, without setting your tail down.

This skater is executing a krooked grind on a hand rail and needs a good olllie to start the trick.

KROOKED GRIND ON A FLAT BAR

The "krooked" is one of the most technical grinds. To do a krooked grind, you have to balance on your front trucks and nose while grinding, so having an ollie to nose manual mastered on a manual pad will help give you the basic motions for this trick.

1. Approach the flat bar backside, and at a slight angle.
2. Pop an ollie and slide your front foot up to the right side of your board's nose.
3. As your front trucks make contact with the bar, straighten out your front leg and press down on your nose. Keep your back knee bent. This should put you in the "krooked" position.

Keeping your back knee bent will make sure your grind stays "krooked." A lower bar is good for learning this style of grind.

4. As you come to the end of the bar, put some extra pressure on your nose, level the board out, and turn off the bar.

50-50 GRIND ON A HANDRAIL

Handrails are one of the most difficult and dangerous skate obstacles. But a lot of skateparks have smaller handrails that are good to learn on. And before you try this trick, make sure you have 50-50s mastered on ledges and flat bars.

1. Roll up to the ledge at a slight angle. As you get closer, spot the exact point on the rail where you plan on landing (usually a little less than halfway down).
2. You need to snap a big ollie to get on the rail, so bend your knees deeply before popping your tail. As you ollie, keep your eyes on your "landing point" on the rail.

PUTTING IT ALL TOGETHER IN A "LINE"

Instead of just doing one single trick, street courses allow you to do a variety of tricks on all sorts of obstacles. It's fun to see how many you can put together in a single "line." Depending on how your street course is set up, you might try a manual on a manual pad, and then grind down a ledge or ollie a gap. It's all up to you, of course—the great thing about skateboarding is that there are no rules and no fixed "routines." The most important thing is to be creative and have fun.

3. Set your trucks down on the rail and stand up straight on your board. Stay on the balls of your feet and your toes to keep your balance.
4. As you reach the end of the handrail, press down slightly on your tail. Bend your knees to absorb the shock as you land back on the ground.

PIVOT TO FAKIE ON A QUARTER-PIPE

The pivot to fakie is a stylish and difficult trick. It's a good set-up trick for more street-oriented tricks where you need to be going backward, like the half-cab boardslide. You should have axle stalls wired before you try this trick (a "pivot" is basically just an axle stall where you balance on your back truck only).

1. Ride up the quarter-pipe the same way you would for an axle stall.
2. As you reach the lip, lift up your front trucks and set your back trucks on the coping. Your hips should rotate so they're parallel with the coping, but unlike in an axle stall, you should keep your upper body and shoulders facing the deck (this makes it easier to come in backward). Balance in this position—on your back truck only—for a just a second or so.
3. When you start to come back in, put some pressure on your back toes to help lift your wheel over the coping. Swivel your hips back around and come back and ride in fakie.
4. Keep your shoulders straight and look over your back shoulder as you ride in and set up for your next trick.

GLOSSARY

180 ollie A trick where you ollie and turn the board 180 degrees to land with your skateboard moving in the opposite position.

50-50 A trick in which both trucks are resting firmly on a ledge.

backside A style associated with any number of tricks in which you turn toward your toes.

bluntslide A trick where you slide with the board resting on a ledge in the position where the wheels are on top of the ledge.

coping Metal piping that is attached to the edge of a ramp to allow for grinds and slides.

fakie Riding a skateboard in a backward position.

flip trick Any number of tricks in which the board flips.

frontside 360 ollie A trick where you ollie then turn a full 360 degrees.

grind Any trick in which the trucks of the skateboard slide across a surface.

half-cab Short for Caballerial, after the skater Steve Caballero who invented it, this trick involves riding fakie and then turning 180 degrees.

kickflip A trick in which the board flips widthwise one full rotation.

line A term used to describe the series of tricks a skater does.

ollie A trick in which a skater jumps with the board by snapping the tail on the ground.

pop shove-it A trick in which the skater ollies and turns 180 degrees while the skater remains in the same position.

slide A trick where the bottom of the skateboard slides across a surface such as a ledge or rail.

tail The upward-curving back end of a skateboard.

truck The part of a skateboard that attaches the wheels to the board.

FOR MORE INFORMATION

Go Skateboarding Foundation
22431 Antonio Parkway
Rancho Santa Margarita, CA 92688
(949) 455-1112
Website: http://goskateboardingfoundation.org
The Go Skateboarding Foundation provides education, career
programming, scholarships, and funding for skateparks.

International Skateboarding Federation (ISF)
P.O. Box 57
Woodward, PA 16882
(814) 883-5635
Website: http://www.internationalskateboardingfederation.com
The International Skateboarding Federation (ISF) is formally
organized and incorporated to provide direction and
governance for the sport of skateboarding worldwide.

Skatelab Indoor Skatepark and Museum
4226 Valley Fair Street
Simi Valley, CA 93063
(805) 578-0040
E-mail: info@skatelab.com
Website: http://www.skatelab.com
Skatelab is a fully functioning enclosed skatepark with
an accompanying museum whose goal it is to display
skateboarding memorabilia and to educate people worldwide
about the history, impact, and reach of the sport.

Skatepark Association of the United States of America (SPAUSA)
2210 Lincoln Boulveard
Venice, CA 90291
Website: http://www.spausa.org
The Skatepark Association of the United States of America
   (SPAUSA) is a nonprofit organization that assists communities
   obtain the resources to build their own skateparks.

Skaters for Public Skateparks
820 North River Street, Loft 206
Portland, OR 97227
Website: http://www.skatepark.org
Skaters for Public Skateparks is a nonprofit advocacy group that
   provides information to those hoping to finance, build, and/or
   improve their local skateparks and other skating venues.

WEBSITES

Because of the changing nature of Internet links, Rosen
Publishing has developed an online list of websites related to the
subject of this book. This site is updated regularly. Please use this
link to access this list:

http://www.rosenlinks.com/STT/course

Brooke, Michael. *The Concrete Wave: The History of Skateboarding.* Toronto, ON: Warwick Publishing, 1999.

Cain, Patrick G. *Skateboarding Street* (Extreme Summer Sports Zone). Minneapolis, MN: Twenty First Century Books, 2013.

Doeden, Matt. *Skateparks: Grab Your Skateboard.* Mankato, MN: Capstone Press, 2002.

Goodfellow, Evan. *Street Skateboarding: Flip Tricks.* Chula Vista, CA: Tracks Publishing, 2005.

Irvine, Alex, and Paul Parker. *So You Think You're a Skateboarder?: 50 Tales from the Street and the Skatepark.* New York, NY: CICO Books, 2014.

Marcus, Ben. *The Skateboard: The Good, the Rad, and the Gnarly.* Minneapolis, MN: MVP Books/Lerner Publishing, 2011.

Michalski, Peter, and Justin Hocking. *Riding Bowls and Pools* (Skateboarding Tips and Tricks). New York, NY: Rosen Publishing, 2016.

Michalski, Peter, and Justin Hocking. *Riding Halfpipes* (Skateboarding Tips and Tricks). New York, NY: Rosen Publishing, 2016.

Powell, Ben. *Skateboarding Skills: The Rider's Guide.* Richmond Hill, Ontario: Firefly Books, 2008.

Sohn, Emily. *Skateboarding: How It Works* (The Science of Sports—Sports Illustrated for Kids). Mankato, MN: Capstone Press, 2010.

Wixon, Ben. *Skateboarding: Instruction, Programming and Park Design.* Champaign, IL: Human Kinetics, 2009.

BIBLIOGRAPHY

Badillo, Steve, and Dan Werner. *Skateboarding: Book of Tricks* (Start-Up Sports) Chula Vista, CA: Tracks Publishing, 2003.

Beal, Becky. *Skateboarding: The Ultimate Guide*. Santa Barbara, CA: ABC-CLIO, 2013.

Hocking, Justin. *Life and Limb: Skateboarders Write from the Deep End*. New York, NY: Soft Skull Press, 2004.

Mullen, Rodney. *The Mutt: How to Skateboard and Not Kill Yourself*. New York, NY: IT Books/HarperCollins, 2004.

Savage, Jeff. *Street Skating: Grinds and Grabs*. Mankato, MN: Capstone Press, 2005.

Wixon, Ben. *Skateboarding: Instruction, Programming and Park Design*. Champaign, IL: Human Kinetics, 2009.

INDEX

A

axle stalls, 30, 39

B

banks, 10, 12, 16, 25
bluntside, 33, 34

C

coping, 23, 30, 31, 39
curbs, 4, 6, 18, 26, 33

F

fakie, 16, 25, 29, 39
50-50, 18, 26, 34, 38
flat bars, 10, 20, 29, 36, 38
Fossil Creek State Park, 12
frontside boardslide, 20
frontside 180 ollie, 24, 32
frontside 360 ollie, 14, 24, 32

H

half-cab boardslide, 29, 39
handrails, 4, 6, 7, 10, 38, 39

K

kickflips, 14, 25, 30, 34
krooked grind, 36

L

ledges, 4, 6, 7, 8, 9, 10, 12, 18, 26, 27,
    30, 33, 34, 38
lines, 13, 38
Louisville Extreme Park, 12
Love Park, 30

M

manual pads, 10, 12, 18, 19, 27, 34,
    36, 38

N

nose manual, 10, 27, 36

O

ollies, 10, 14, 15, 16, 18, 19, 20, 24,
    25, 26, 27, 29, 32, 34, 36, 38

P

pyramids, 10, 12, 14, 15, 16, 24, 25,
    32, 33
pivots, 39

Q

quarter-pipes, 8, 9, 10, 12, 21, 23, 30,
    31, 39

R

rails, 8, 10, 20, 38, 39
Rye Airfield, 12

S

S.K.A.T.E., 21
skateboard trivia, 29–30
Skate Park of Tampa (S.P.O.T.), 12
skateparks, 4, 6, 7, 8, 10, 12, 13, 21,
    38
street contests, 8, 12
street courses
    advanced tricks for, 32–39
    basic tricks for, 15–23
    benefits of, 7–8
    elements of, 10
    intermediate tricks for, 24–31
    and safety, 8, 13

T

tailslide, 26
trucks, 16, 18, 19, 20, 23, 27, 30, 31,
    36, 39

ABOUT THE AUTHORS

Peter Michalski is a young adult nonfiction author who has penned many instructional titles for teens, covering sports, careers, and health issues.

Justin Hocking lives and skateboards in New York City. He is also an editor of the book *Life and Limb: Skateboarders Write from the Deep End*, published in 2004 by Soft Skull Press.

PHOTO CREDITS

Cover (skateboarder) Jeff Gross/Getty Images; cover (background) Thomas Barwick/Taxi/Getty Images; pp. 1, 6, 11, 14, 24, 32 Timothy Lee Lantgen/Shutterstock.com; p. 3 Dizzo/Vetta/ Getty Images; pp. 4-5 mgs/Moment Open/Getty Images; p. 5 (inset) Colorblind/Photodisc/Getty Images; p. 7 Tony Garcia/ Image Source/Getty Images; p. 9 International Rescue/The Image Bank/Getty Images; p. 15 Chris Cheadle/All Canada Photos/ Getty Images; p. 17 © Joe Tree/Alamy Stock Photo; p. 19 © Zoonar GmbH/Alamy Stock Photo; p. 22 © simon evans/Alamy Stock Photo; p. 26 Daniel Milchev/Stone/Getty Images; p. 28 © Mike Sivyer/Alamy Stock Photo; p. 31 Thomas Barwick/Iconica/ Getty Images; p. 33 Ty Allison/The Image Bank/Getty Images; p. 35 Wavebreakmedia/iStock/Thinkstock; p. 36 Keith Ladzinski/ Aurora/Getty Images; p. 37 Ryan McVay/Photodisc/Thinkstock; back cover, interior pages (bricks) Ensuper/Shutterstock.com; interior pages banner textures Naburalna/Shutterstock.com

Designer: Michael Moy; Editor: Philip Wolny;
Photo Researcher: Karen Huang and Philip Wolny